HARTLEPOOL
COLLEGE OF FURTHER EDUCATION

24 7NT

ᘓ Steve Fenton and Azra Sadiq were the researchers
on this project. They work at the Centre for the Study
of Minorities and Social Change in the Department of
Sociology at Bristol University. Azra Sadiq carried out
the interviews. Charles Watters advised on the
service and policy implications of the research.

Any further enquiries about the research should
be made to Steve Fenton.

© **Commission for Racial Equality**
Elliot House
10-12 Allington Street
London SW1E 5EH

First published in 1993
ISBN 1 85442 087 9
Price: £ 2.50
Printed by College Hill Press Ltd

Contents

Foreword 5

Introduction 7

Voices of Sorrow 13

It all began when ... 15

What made it worse ... 23

Someone to turn to ... 32

The Inner City Mental Health Project 37

Recommendations 41

Foreword

The Commission for Racial Equality funded this research study of sixteen Asian women in Bristol who had suffered from depression, in order to examine the assumptions on which much social policy on ethnic minorities in Britain has been based. Two of these have had serious consequences for very basic service provision – first, the widely-held view that people from non-western cultures do not experience depression as a psychological condition; and second that, in any case, they 'look after their own' and do not need help from public services.

The study was based on intensive interviews with the women in their own language. We are grateful to them for being prepared to share painful experiences with the researchers. The accounts show that all of them had a good understanding of their condition. Some felt unable to turn to their families for help. If they did not discuss the underlying reason for their suffering with their GPs, this was partly because they did not speak English well enough. They had no such problem if there was an Asian helper at the practice.

The study reveals the extent to which the women's depression was intensified by their difficulties as immigrants. Without family or friends of their own to turn to in a crisis, they found that their complaints to the council about intolerable housing conditions and persistent racial aggression by their white neighbours, which often kept them prisoners in their own homes, usually fell on deaf ears. There was little support available to help them in their distress.

Local authorities and health providers have a duty to provide services for all the communities in their area, whatever their size, and to see that they take account of their different cultural and linguistic needs. The study makes a number of recommendations, and the CRE urges all health and social services providers to give urgent priority to the task of developing and improving services for their ethnic minority clients.

Sir Michael Day
Chair, Commission for Racial Equality

Introduction

T he limited provision made for ethnic minority communities by social services departments and health providers has been a matter of long-standing concern to the CRE. This booklet focuses on a particular area of need which, for various reasons, has gone largely unheeded.

In 1989, the CRE agreed to fund a research study by Steve Fenton and Azra Sadiq of South Asian women in Bristol who had suffered from depression. Sixteen women were interviewed in depth, in their own language. They talked openly, and at great length, about their experiences – 'how it all began', their thoughts and feelings, and how they coped or, in many cases, did not. The women also spoke of all the things that had made their 'illness' worse: being migrants in a country where they did not feel accepted or wanted; the problems of not speaking the language; the loneliness of having no immediate family or friends of their own; the unremitting racial hostility of neighbours and white people generally; and the official indifference to their complaints and problems.

The interviews contribute to dispelling some of the myths about Asians and other ethnic minority communities which have shaped so much social policy in this area:

- The idea that they 'look after their own' through the extended family structure and community networks, and therefore do not need help from public services.

- The belief that people from non-western cultures do not experience depression as a psychological condition, because the importance of religion and community values gives them a different understanding of themselves as individuals.

- The claim that people from non-western cultures do not fully understand, or cannot express, their feelings, and that they only talk about their physical symptoms.

It should be made clear at the outset that the project was never intended to be a statistical survey using a large sample and short, superficial interviews. The validity of the findings lies precisely in the depth of the interviews, and the fact that the 16 women, contacted through a health centre, a language class, and the Inner City Mental Health Project (ICMHP) team in Bristol, told their stories in their own way, without any inhibitions, to a bilingual researcher for an average of about ten hours each. Although no assessment or diagnostic measures were used, the study draws a clear picture of the 'precipitating factors' of the illness, and of the 'background, exacerbating or vulnerability factors' which affected the women's ability to cope with it.

A key question must be how much we can learn from such a small, localised study. The women were all from particular ethnic groups in the Indian subcontinent, with distinct economic, social and cultural histories. All but one were born in India or Pakistan, and had come to Britain as young adults. Most had been here for about ten years, although a few had arrived quite recently. Most of the women were Muslims, but there were also a few Sikhs and Hindus. However, so long as one is careful not to use the interviews to make sweeping generalisations about all Asian women in Britain, the study should be extremely valuable – there is enough evidence from other studies that many of the experiences which the women from Bristol talked about are shared by Asian women elsewhere in Britain.

Depression, or just life?

In the language of western psychiatric medicine, the term 'depression' is used to describe a specific mental and emotional state with particular symptoms, and is treated, in part, by anti-depressant drugs. This does not mean, however, that there is absolute clarity about what exactly depression is, or what causes it, or the best way of treating it. Indeed, it is often argued that there is no real distinction between someone who cannot deal with life's pressures and someone who is ill with depression, between 'minor' and 'major' depression. No-one is sure when, or whether, this condition can be called an illness – at least not without clearly defining what they mean by illness. If the specialists are in disarray about this, it seems pointless to argue about whether the women in the study were truly suffering from depression. Hardly any of them used the word, and most were probably unaware of it.

But we can be sure of one thing; the women whom Azra Sadiq spoke to described symptoms which, if they had been described to their GPs by English speakers, would have been diagnosed as 'depression' – the women spoke of weakness, listlessness, and tearfulness; they were unable to sleep; they could not cope with the simplest things; they lost their sense of self-confidence and the meaning of life; and they contemplated suicide as a way out. All eight symptoms were mentioned by a majority of the women, most mentioned six or more symptoms, and none mentioned fewer than five.

While their suffering always began as a completely natural and normal response to some terrible personal shock, like the death of a close relative back in India or Pakistan, this turned into a virtually unmanageable state of mental and emotional distress which the women invariably described as a kind of illness, not ordinary illness like rheumatism or arthritis, but an illness which took over their lives and trapped them, a kind of 'thought sickness' – *soochne ke bimaari*. As one of them said, 'My sorrow has become my illness'.

The question of whether the women were suffering from clinical depression or not cannot be resolved here. But there is no doubt that they were in great emotional and mental turmoil, and very unwell. What the interviews did show, again and again, was the fact that the women were fully aware of what was happening to them, and clearly understood their condition as an illness of the mind – not madness, which was seen as a more acute form of psychological illness (although they realised that their thought-sickness could drive them that way if it was allowed to go on). They expressed themselves lucidly and eloquently, and if they did only talk to their GPs about their physical symptoms, this was because they did not think a doctor could do anything about the real cause of their illness. The women did not believe that vitamins or sleeping tablets were the real solution – as one woman drily remarked, 'this is a thinking sickness, not a sleeping sickness'. Another echoed this when she said that her doctor's telling her not to think so much was like saying, 'don't be ill'. But, most importantly, even if they had wanted to talk about their real troubles with the doctor, this was out of the question because of the language problem; the women had little hesitation in unburdening themselves to the Asian teamworker from the Inner City Mental Health Project.

The interviews also made it plain that the women were beset by various other problems in their lives which made things much worse – some of them familiar to anyone bringing up children on their own. The problem of isolation which the women faced when their worlds were turned upside down as a result of unhappy relationships or broken marriages was acutely intensified by their inability to speak English, the fact that they had no family or friends of their own in this country, their ignorance about medical, welfare and housing provision, their unfamiliarity with the ways of officialdom, severe economic hardship, and the semi-permanent state of quarantine they imposed on themselves and their children through constant fear of racial harassment and attack. In many cases, it was the strain of coping simultaneously on all these fronts that made it so much harder to come to terms with whatever it was that was preoccupying them.

The women spoke of deaths in their immediate family, disloyal husbands, and family disputes. There was nothing typically 'Asian' about the tragedies and conflicts they described. Yet, possibly, an English person might find it difficult to understand that someone should be so shattered by the fact that her husband sold her jewellery, or so distressed that a father-in-law's new wife and family did not think well of her. The cultural norms and values by which Asian

women are brought up in India and Pakistan are significantly different from those that shape life in western societies. Whether or not
Asian women in Britain live in extended families – and one study[1]
suggests that only 16 per cent do – aunts, uncles, grandparents, and
relatives-in-law are important players in their lives and have much
more influence than their counterparts in western families.
Furthermore, as the interviews suggest, life in Asian households can
be just as stressed as in western ones, with members of the family
lining up on one side or the other when there is a dispute. In one
case, the woman turned into a family and social outcast overnight
when her husband asked her to take the four children and leave the
house, even though *she* had done nothing wrong.

While some of the symptoms of depression can be treated with
vitamins, sleeping pills, etc, others, like feelings of despair and personal inadequacy, grow out of expectations that have been shaped by
psychological, cultural and social conditions. Unless social workers,
GPs, and counsellors have some awareness and understanding of the
different upbringings their ethnic minority clients and patients
might have had, it is unlikely that they will be able to give them
much help.

What this study makes clear is the real suffering which women
from certain ethnic minority groups experience as a consequence
of policies founded on stereotypes and lack of information. The last
chapter makes a number of basic recommendations for health
providers and local authority housing and social services
departments.

[1] Colin Brown (1984), *Black and White in Britain: The Third PSI Report*, Policy
Studies Institute, London: Gower.

Voices of
Sorrow

'... I ask Allah if I'll always be like this ...
what sort of life is this? ...
I can't look after myself or my family ...
my children are here and there ...
this is no good ... I'd be better off
dead than like this.'

It all began when...

All the women could point to the exact moment when their lives began to unravel. Often, 'it all began when ... ' a close member of their family died back home, or when there were problems with their husbands or in-laws.

❧ A death in the family

The pain and grief of losing someone you love can seem like the end of the world when it happens. For some of the women, it was as though they had lost their loved ones twice over, once when they left their countries, and then when their mothers, fathers, sisters or brothers died. This was a different sort of parting, though, and they had to come to terms with it on their own, far away from home.

For many, the news usually came too late to travel back, even if they could afford this. The shock was made worse by the helplessness the women felt being miles away; it was as if things might have been different, somehow, if they'd been there. For some, not knowing what was actually happening to their dying relatives, moment by moment, became a terrible ache.

Most of the women turned to their faith for help in accepting what had happened, but even this solace was only partial, cut off as they were from the customary rites and mourning ceremonies that help those who are left behind to reconcile themselves to their loss.

Very few people here, even the women's husbands and children, knew their families back home; there might be sympathy, but they could never fully understand. Talking about the past, about their loss, was the only way they might learn to remember differently, but for many of the women this simple remedy was not available. Torn between their need to remember, and the mounting pressures on them to forget, some just stopped trying to juggle between the two and lost themselves in their own world, brooding endlessly. Three of the women could not 'pull themselves together' enough to cope, and had to be hospitalised.

All the women were intensely aware of their distress, and the way it consumed their lives, leaving them almost paralysed in the face of urgent responsibilities and claims.

Sunita[2] lost her brother about two years earlier and was stunned by the blow. She never saw him before he died –

> I know he only had so long to live, but for me there's a place in my heart that's empty ... my life was thrown into sorrow (*ghum*). People say, 'You must be patient', but how can I be patient when my sorrow has become an illness? I ask myself if I'm going to be like this all my life.

Mounira was older than the other women, and this made her feel less able to cope with shock. She was with her husband in Pakistan when he died, but it was the more recent loss of her nephew in a tragic accident that devastated her. The boy had been like a son to her, and she was here in England when it happened.

> ... It was God's will. The roof of the cave just fell in on him. Someone else also died with him. I can't forget his death, even now. I feel it in my heart (*dil*). When you're young you can take these things more easily, but not when your blood gets weak from the fears (*fikar*) and illness. There's ordinary illness, and there's the illness of sorrow. I don't sleep very well. I can't forget everything that's happened, even though I want to ... I keep telling myself, and everyone else also tells me, to forget the past. But some things are beyond your control. That's why I can say that I am old now.

Sushila's first blow came when her husband walked out on her and the children. She had no family of her own here, and fell very ill. Then, when her sister died, there was no-one to turn to:

> My heart was like a sieve. I couldn't stop thinking about all that had

---

[2] The names used are not the women's real names.

happened ... The pain got worse. My head went round and round in circles. It was worse because I didn't actually get the news till a week after it happened, and they'd had the funeral by then. I know that I probably couldn't have got there in time anyway, but the thing was that I was here when she died, going on as if nothing had happened.

❧ Unhappy relationships

While western cultures give a lot of importance to people as individuals, Asian traditions set greater store by people's relationships with others, and mostly those with their family and community. A breakdown in family relationships is a threat to the roles by which individuals define themselves, and can cause tremendous mental and emotional turmoil.

Quite apart from her loss of self-esteem when her husband left her and the children, Sushila lost the context within which she understood herself, as woman, mother, and member of the community. There was also the very real loss of a circle of friends and relatives in a country she had come to as someone's wife, the pressure of making ends meet, and being solely responsible for bringing up her children in an unfamiliar and often hostile environment.

Jaswinder was 56 years old. Her ordeal began when her husband told her to take the four children and leave the house. It was like the end of her world; everyone she knew seemed to be avoiding her, all her husband's relatives, and everyone who knew her story. As a single mother, she felt it was always her morality that was being questioned by people, never mind how much her husband was to blame.

> It was a time of sorrow and anxiety . I thought I was going mad (*paagl*)... that's why they sent me to hospital ... I've been in this country for nearly sixteen years now, and to be honest, it's only now that there's a little happiness in my heart. When I came here from Pakistan it was hard, what with young children and not knowing anybody or anything. My husband wasn't too bad then, but suddenly one day he just told me to leave his house ... I was stunned. I didn't know what to say, or where to go. I have no relatives in England, let alone here in Bristol. His relatives all took his side and didn't even want to see us.

Jaswinder finally turned to someone from her village in Pakistan. The man took her and the children in, in spite of the inconvenience, and went out of his way to help them.

> ... you know how difficult it is living in someone else's place. I don't have anyone even now, but at the time I felt utterly and hopelessly alone ... My friend did a lot of running around for me. I didn't really know what was happening ... I couldn't eat or sleep for all the worries. I just thought in my heart, agonised about what was happening, and about what to do.

Jaswinder became stronger in time, 'by Allah's grace', but she now suffers from thrombosis, which she thinks is much easier to bear -

> ... It's a different sort of illness ... an illness of the blood. My blood gets frozen. The doctors say I have to keep taking tablets for the rest of my life – but at least I'm happy in every other way. Then, there was no happiness in my life – you wouldn't wish what happened to me on anyone.

Amina's depression began when her husband threw her out and she had to rent a room as a single Asian woman. In a community where living in a family is the norm, a single, married woman living on her own can all too easily become an object of malicious gossip. Amina was renting a room from an (Asian) family, and used to spend some time after work in the communal lounge watching TV or talking before going to her bedroom. But the family's attitude suddenly changed, and Amina could find no explanation for it.

> I used to be alright. I talked to the woman quite a bit, and it was nice to have someone to come home to after work. Then they started to change. They didn't want to talk to me as much, and when I came into the room they would leave and turn off the TV. I come home from work now and go straight to my room after eating, even though I'd like to watch some TV and chat a bit. I read or write letters, but I feel trapped in my room. ... If I've done something wrong, I wish they'd tell me, but they don't say anything, so it's very difficult and makes me feel even worse. At least at work I can talk to people, and maybe laugh. I come here and I'm alone.

The common stereotype about Asian families is that they 'look after their own'. This is largely because of the extended family structure prevalent in the Indian subcontinent. Seen as tightly-knit and unfailing support structures, Asian households have been overlooked by health and social services departments when planning their services.

In the first place, only 16 per cent of Asian households in Britain[3] are extended families. Secondly, they are far from being as close-knit and trouble-free as they are thought to be. As in any family, there can be tensions and stresses, with everyone taking one side or another in an argument or dispute. Occasionally, individual members of the family can become very isolated, and feel victimised and shunned.

Migration necessarily divides families, but this has been exacerbated in Britain by the increasingly restrictive immigration controls applied to particular ethnic groups. It can take many heart-breaking years before a family is allowed to be reunited – or not, as the case may be. Moreover, since the introduction of visas for all countries in the Indian subcontinent, and an ever-increasing number of African countries, even holiday visits have been made more difficult for nationals of these countries.

Many of the women had few family members nearby – some had none. Also, they did not have much chance of making friends with other South Asian women, and those who did not speak English were even more socially isolated. Some of them said that when they did go out, there was always the dread of being followed and taunted with being 'Pakis'. This also deterred women with young children from going to the park, and they were confined to playing in the garden – usually a very small one, if they had one at all. The thought of moving to somewhere better was offset by the prospect of having to face down new neighbours, losing the support of the community where they were, and the distance from Asian shops.

Shahnaz's problems went back to the time her father-in-law

---

[3] Brown, *op cit.*.

remarried. She had the feeling that her new relatives did not really accept her, that they thought she was unworthy. She felt desperately lonely, and longed for support.

> ... I get frightened, and it feels as though there's a ball rolling round in my stomach. I'm terrified that something bad is going to happen. I think constantly in my heart. Sometimes it all gets too much, and my heart sinks and my stomach surges, and my head feels as though it will burst from the pressure. I'm always apologising to my husband for being like this, but I can't help it, it just happens. ... I start crying, and cannot stop myself, even when the children are there, and they get upset – they're still very young. I keep telling myself that I must live for them, that if I don't, there's no-one else to look after them.

Once, Shahnaz's father-in-law rang, and she felt he was cold to her. She couldn't stop thinking about it, and yearned for her own family, her parents and her brothers and sisters, to share her troubles with them.

> All I do is sit inside these four walls. My husband is good to me, and we do talk, but it's not the same as your mother or brother or sister. He says I worry too much, but I can't help it. I do all this thinking in my heart. I know it affects the brain, but what can I do?

Shahida told us that her illness began when her husband and his brother had a row about the ownership of their house. They had bought the place jointly, both putting in a lot of hard-earned money for the deposit. The brother took care of the business side, as he had more experience in these matters. Shahida and her husband then moved into the house, and put in a lot of work to improve it. A year or two later, her husband decided to sell the house and recoup his share. But his brother disputed his stake, saying the house was his – legally, it was in his name.

> ... The two brothers almost had a fight. It was a very bad time for us, and that's when I started to get ill. In those six months I lost a lot of weight and became very weak. I used to worry a lot, and spent days and nights just thinking and thinking in my heart about it all, about what would happen. Sometimes they'd have big arguments in the

house, and I'd feel even worse. The life would just go out of my heart.

Nasreen was a young woman whose troubles began about the time her parents tried to arrange her marriage. The arrangements had gone quite well, and both sets of parents and the couple had accepted everything happily. But things began to go wrong, and the engagement was broken off. Nasreen could not shake off her depression, and it started affecting her work, an added worry.

> ... I just feel very sad. I can't laugh any more. I seem to cry all the time. I can't eat properly and I'm losing weight. I get very tired in the day, but I can't sleep at night. And now my work is suffering. The other day I sent a whole lot of wrong letters out and my supervisor spoke to me about it. Everyone at work has noticed a change in me. I used to talk a lot before ... I see others laughing, and ask myself what there is to laugh about. Only my supervisor knows, and she's quite good and understanding. I don't mind going to work, it's better than staying at home. At home I do nothing, just stay in my room and think and think and cry.

Yasmin was 28 years old, and had three children. Her husband had been out of work for eight years, and had reached the point where he had lost the will to work, or find work. He spent most of his day wandering around aimlessly, and did very little to support the family. Yasmin had no choice but to start working herself at a drycleaning firm. But her illness really began the day her husband stole her jewellery and sold it to raise money for himself – some Asian families place a lot of importance on having jewellery to pass on to their daughters, or as a form of investment. Certainly, for Yasmin, the jewellery had great personal and social significance, and she found it very difficult to reconcile herself to the loss.

> My illness has been with me for quite a long time – about a year and a half – and I'm still not better. A year ago, though, I was very ill. It all started when my husband took all my jewellery and sold it. I was shattered. I thought my heart had stopped, like I was going to die – the jewellery was all I had. I still think about it in my heart, even now, and my head aches from it. You won't believe it, but it actually

feels like it will burst ... it's the nerve on the side of the forehead.

Farida was a young, 24-year-old who had been in Britain for only three years. She had two young children and, apart from her husband, had no relatives of her own here. Her husband's family lived quite far away, and, as he was unemployed, they could not afford to visit them very often. For the same reason, Farida could not think about visiting her family in Pakistan. Her depression was the natural consequence of intense loneliness and homesickness.

> ... When I came here, that first day, everything seemed very strange to me. Where we live in Pakistan there's a lot of coming and going. You see everybody. Here, once you're inside these four walls it's like you're in prison, you don't see anyone or speak to anyone ... I guess my illness began when I came here. My heart wasn't in this country. It makes me very low being here on my own, alone with my thoughts, and always thinking. I try to think about other things, but it doesn't work; my thoughts always come back to my sadness. Being alone makes me terribly anxious. I can't even talk to my husband about it, because he just tells me to stop thinking so much, that it's bad for me. I know it's making me ill, but I can't help it. Sometimes I just sit by the fire, and a whole day passes and I can't do anything, no work or anything .

What made it worse...

❧ Racial hostility

All the women had experienced racial hostility and abuse, from snubs and sneers to open aggression by neighbours and others in public places. Suffering from an illness whose basic symptoms are insecurity and withdrawal, the fear of racial violence further intensified the women's feelings of persecution.

Their greatest anxiety was for their children's safety. Most of the women recounted incidents of racial bullying, abuse or attack, in parks, in the street and elsewhere, and they spoke of the dread they lived in all the time of 'what might happen'. They were afraid to let their children walk home from school, or play in the local park, lest they be set upon, or called names, or threatened. This meant the children were mostly kept cooped up at home, where there was little space to play, and both mother and child missed out on fresh air, exercise and outdoor enjoyment.

Some of the women described the racial aggression they had experienced from neighbours when they moved into a predominantly white area. In three cases the women had moved out of an area with a well-established ethnic minority population to parts of Bristol where they were the first, or among the very first, black or Asian families. One had moved to accept an offer of a council home, while the others were looking for better housing. What is disturbing is the fact that racial hostility and harassment are surfacing in 'new' areas of Bristol which, until recently, had been almost exclusively white.

Shahnaz's anxieties about what her new in-laws might do to discredit her were compounded by her fear of being attacked or robbed.

> ... I'm afraid that something bad is going to happen, so I don't go out
> on my own at all. ... If I have to go to the clinic, I wait for my husband.

He works in a restaurant and this means he is home most mornings. But he's away from the house from half-past-two in the afternoon till two or three in the morning. I'm in a state of terror all that time. I lock all the doors and the windows when he leaves – there are a lot of people around here prepared to do that, you know – English and black people. We're always afraid of them. We rarely take the children to the park. We just go into the garden when the weather is fine.

Najma and her husband had been about to move out of Westborough to a 'new' part of Bristol, but he died in an accident. Najma went ahead with the move on her own. It wasn't long before she was faced with a deputation of neighbours telling her to 'go back to where she came from' – the last thing she needed when she was still in a state of shock and grief.

> ... It's a nice house, nicely decorated and things like that ... but it's far from our shops and the doctors ... all our friends and relations are in Westborough, so I feel all alone here. ... It (racial hostility) didn't used to bother me before – we'd mind our own business and they got on with theirs. But here – my God! – people like this shouldn't be allowed to exist. Our neighbours are so bad I don't know what to do.

Kulsum had been having problems with her husband, and was tormented by the thought that he might leave her. They had moved out of Westborough when the council relocated them to Northborough, an area where there are very few Asian families. To top it all, the neighbours were making her life miserable. The children of a friend who lived nearby had been hit and abused, and rubbish had been pushed through her letter box.

> ... We've had a lot of problems since we moved here – it's that sort of area. Take the family across the road. When we first moved here they seemed alright; they came over and said hello. Then, the whole family, especially the man, seemed to be watching our house all the time to see what we were doing. I could tell they were watching us because they would be at their window, till they realised we had seen them...
>
> About a month later, we had a visit from the social security people. They said that my husband was working and claiming benefit at the same

time, and that someone had told them about his movements. It then started to make sense why the people across the road had been watching us. My husband explained that, yes, he did do some work, but he always told the social security office about it. In any case, he hadn't done any work for a long time now. They accepted this.

But the people across the road still keep snooping on us. It's like a prison here, you can't do anything without that man watching you. He came over once and told me to not to let my children play outside because he didn't like it. He's always watching them when they come home from school, and this terrifies me, because you don't know what these people might do. Now I don't let the children play outside, and always pick them up from school myself, because he started making horrible faces at them and frightening them.

Ayesha lived in a council property. When the neighbours started harassing her family, she reported it to the council, but they did nothing.

Just before last Christmas, we put a gate on our side of the back garden so that the children couldn't go out into the road. The next day we found the gate in the next door's garden; they had taken it down and put it on their side of the fence where there was a gap. I went to ask for our gate back, but they said it was theirs, and that I was lying. They were very rude, and called us all sorts of names, like Paki. So I got in touch with the council to report them as racists, because that's what I think they are. The council did nothing. I daren't let the children out in the front because the people across the road scare them, and at the back their toys are taken away and they are called names. I really hate living here ...

Ayesha moved out of the area when she managed to arrange an exchange with an old lady in Leicester.

Kuldip had been living in a small council flat with her young son and elderly mother ever since her separation from her husband. Racial taunts and harassment were daily events in her life.

... There are some in the block who don't look kindly on our sort. It wasn't very long ago that I bought my son this bike, and he went out on it in the passage – I thought it was alright if he just went up and down a little. Then I heard him screaming. I ran out to find all these English children around him, hitting him, and they'd thrown his bike over the side of the flats. When they saw me, they just started calling me nasty names. This went on for about five or ten minutes, when a black lady who lives in the end flat came to my rescue and told them all off. It was only then that they went away. She is good to me, and helps me a lot. She then went down and got the bike and said that if there was any more trouble I was to call her.

Shahida's misery over the feud between her husband and her brother-in-law about the ownership of their house (see p 20) was the main cause of her depression, but there were countless other problems dragging her down – they had moved to another part of Bristol where there were fewer Asians; it was very difficult to keep in touch with all her old friends; she spoke very little English and didn't feel confident enough to make any English friends; and, although the house was immaculate and in a very beautiful area near a park, the neighbours were unfriendly, and she was increasingly afraid of being attacked.

... I would sometimes wander around the house aimlessly, forgetting what I was meant to be doing. My memory just went. I didn't go out very much. It wasn't the same living there; you couldn't just pop in to see someone. I had to get a bus to Westborough, and the journey there and back could take the good part of a day. I used to get so tired. I didn't have the strength to wait around for buses ... So, I spent most of my time inside the house.

... I used to go to (English) classes, and still want to. They were a chance to talk a little to our own women, as well as learn – but the mini bus doesn't come out this far.

... When we first moved here, the next door neighbours used to give us nasty looks, and their children would hit our children, so I kept them indoors. They used to say our house smelled when we cooked, and all sorts of horrible things like that. But, thank God, they moved away soon afterwards. The ones who came after them are alright, they mind their own business and we mind ours. But there aren't any other Asians in this area, and we do feel afraid. We are surrounded by English people, and if anything were to happen, who would we go to? They say there are a lot of burglaries in this area ...

🍂 Looking after the children

Many of the women had young children to look after. What should have been a joy became a terrible responsibility because of their poor health. Almost all the women reported symptoms of general weakness and tiredness, and described how impossible it was to cope with the everyday business of living. Not surprisingly, the problem of looking after children was more acute when the women had sole responsibility for the children because their husbands had walked out on them.

Women with older children also talked about the worries they had about their children's education, and their prospects of finding a good job. All the women were keen to see their children do well in their studies. One had a daughter who was about to start at a polytechnic and, while she welcomed her daughter's achievements, she was against the idea of her moving to another city. The mothers who were learning English thought that this would help them to understand, and get on with, their children better, as well as help them with their school work.

Then there was the problem of arranging marriages for the children. When Jaswinder and her four children were forced by her husband to fend for themselves, she was left with the worry of arranging good marriages for her daughters. Even though it was her husband who had abandoned her, it was Jaswinder's reputation that suffered.

Bringing up children is a big responsibility for all parents, but these women were unwell and needed help themselves. Some were able to turn to their husbands, but those who did not have this option found themselves in a desperate situation.

Yasmin's husband did not like the idea of her working at the drycleaning company, but he did not do much about finding a job himself, and there was no alternative. Nor could she depend on him to help at home or with the children. Then there were all the social obligations – attending weddings and seeing that the children were well-dressed, because otherwise 'people would talk'.

> I have two daughters, one three years old and the other five. I have to

think of them, and save for them. You can't say what's going to happen. Look at me and how my fate (*kismet*) has turned out with him. But money is always a problem ... I can barely manage the household expenses nowadays, let alone save. But I have faith in Rab, and we'll see what happens ... The biggest problem is when I'm working a shift, from 3.30 pm, and they (the children) are sometimes left on their own. My husband is supposed to look after them, but he comes in late from his wanderings.

The women also talked about the worries they had about their children being influenced by western ideas.

... the children go out late at night and drink and smoke. Never mind the boys, but the girls too, they 'do fashion' like the English. They cut their hair and wear English clothes and use make-up ...

'Doing fashion' was a phrase often used to describe the way the younger generation was being swayed by western culture. There was also some concern about the diminishing role of religion in their children's lives.

... religion and Islam come second with a lot of the younger children. For some it's because their parents don't keep them in control, and for others – what can the parents do if their children mix with the wrong sort – a lot of them go to pubs and clubs.

The idea that ethnic minority families are torn by intergenerational conflict is a false generalisation. There may be serious differences in some cases, but religious and cultural traditions are happily preserved in many families, with parents and children reaching a compromise.

❧ Housing problems

About half the women had problems with their housing. They did not talk about their housing conditions as the primary factor in their 'illness', but various aspects of their housing situation affected their well-being – run-down, dilapidated houses lacking basic amenities like running hot and cold water, and in urgent need of repair; the hopeless task of getting the council or landlord to make improvements; difficult stairs for women who had asthma or arthritis; lack of a garden when the public park was a dangerous place; and unpleasant encounters with neighbours who did nothing to conceal their hostility towards Asians.

Salma had been widowed twice, and now believed that people were plotting against her. At the same time, she was in desperate straits, living with her four children in a small, crumbling, two-bedroomed terraced house. She had no money for repairs, and no husband to support her or help put things right.

> ... When we moved here – from one pit to another – I left all my furniture behind. We live like animals here.

There was little wallpaper in any of the rooms. The geyser was broken and there was only cold water in the bathroom. To have a bath, Salma had to heat water on the cooker downstairs and carry it up. The plumbing needed repair, and there was no water in the cold water tap of the washbasin. Salma slept with her daughter in one of the bedrooms and her three sons slept in the other. One of the downstairs rooms could not be used because it needed replastering, and the floor boards were dangerous in another.

> ... Yes, we've applied for a repair grant, but that was about a year and a half ago. They came and took pictures and didn't do anything about it. You know what these people are like, they just see us and turn away. I don't understand it. We've also applied for a council house, but they say it will take a long time ... You asked about my health, where do I start? There's nothing wrong with me, just nerves ... I feel like my life is being squeezed out of me.

Then there was the worry about her children. They could not play outside or go to the park, 'because the English children fought with them', and the house was too small and dangerous to play in.

Yasmin's depression about her jewellery was exacerbated by the state of her house.

> There's a lot of damp ... it needs decorating and replastering ... I come

back very tired from work and then have to do the housework, cook-ing, cleaning and things like papering. I've applied for a council place, but I've been on the waiting list for two years now. They keep saying that I haven't got enough points. I don't know how many points they want or how I get them, and I don't have the time to go and talk to them. I suppose there's one shift when I could go, but then I'd have to find someone who speaks English and ask them to go with me ... It's almost like begging ... but what can we do?

Kuldip's problems with her neighbours were made worse by her fears for her family's health.

... The flat itself is very damp. As you know, both my mother and I have asthma, so it just gets worse. And the stairs to the flat, and in the flat itself, are all too much for my mother sometimes. The other day she wasn't feeling well and fell halfway down the stairs. As you see, the front door is straight ahead, and her head just went through the pane in the door. She was lucky. With God's blessings, she just had a little cut, but it could have killed her. Mercifully, the lady next door phoned the council and they are coming to fix it; otherwise I would have had to take someone with me and go there myself.

... I've applied for another place, and asked them for a house. I don't like living in a flat. If it was a proper street, and something hap-pened, someone might see and help, but here you're in a corner where no-one can see you. Also, I'd like a bit of garden, because I can't keep taking my little boy out – he says he's bored inside, so we go for walks down Market Street, which is okay, but this part here around the flats is frightening. And then the stairs aren't good. I get very frightened living here. That's why my mother is living with me, but she is old and couldn't do much if something happened.

Jamila's depression began because of her worsening relationship with her husband, but she also suffered from arthritis and couldn't cope with the stairs.

We've applied for a council house, but of course it's taking a long time. The doctor has written a letter saying that it's bad for me to be living here, but they still haven't done anything about it. It's been about two years now ... the pain is becoming unbearable and I'm getting more and more anxious ... It's not just the stairs, although that's what's important at the moment – the house is also damp and that makes everyone else ill too. I don't know how long I'll be able to go on like this. It's very painful. And then the problems when my husband is at home make it even worse ... because he just has arguments with me and the children. There's a lot of bad feeling in the house and it all makes me feel very sad.

Many of the women mentioned difficulties with speaking and reading English, especially if their husbands had left them and they had to sort out their housing problems on their own. Dealing with complex and usually unsympathetic bureaucracies is a problem for everyone, but the women who had been left by their husbands or forced out of their homes were confronted with it all of a sudden, as a matter of extreme urgency. Few of them had dealt with the authorities before, they were unfamiliar with the system, and, worst of all, they did not understand English well enough.

Jaswinder's friend from her village in Pakistan took her and her four children in when they were homeless, but he had his own family, three of Jaswinder's children were over sixteen years old, and there were only two bedrooms in the house. Jaswinder could not speak English herself, but her children could. She was at a loss as to what to do to find somewhere to live, and to sort out money matters. The community social worker was the one who finally helped her to approach the housing department and to arrange her finances.

Help like this was invaluable, but it was hard to come by, and the women often did not know where to turn. Advice and assistance with housing would have a substantial and beneficial effect on their lives, and could possibly be provided through health centres.

Someone to turn to...

❧ GPs and Social Services

All but one of the 16 women had visited their GP. They did not necessarily talk about their problem in psychological terms, but concentrated on symptoms such as sleeplessness, loss of weight, and aches and pains. It was very clear that the women knew exactly what their problem was, but in most cases they were reluctant to talk about it openly to their GP – they did not think a doctor could do much to help. Kuldip thought that she would do better to go back home and see a religious healer –

> If you ask me truthfully, I don't know what to do ... What should I do? Go on taking anti-depressants or go to Pakistan?

Ayesha was the only one who did not see her GP –

> I didn't go to the doctor about my trouble, because there was nothing she could do for me. I get a lot of different ailments – aches and pains, and tiredness – and I just take Panadols. I don't think I'll get well till my husband stops seeing that other woman. Hopefully, the move to Leicester will be better for us all.

Salma saw her GP with a linkworker, because she did not speak much English. She told him about the aches in her body and a sense of constriction all over, which made her feel very tired and unable to do her usual chores in the house. But it was after her consultation with the GP that she told the linkworker that she thought people were conspiring against her, and that this was upsetting her dreadfully, and making it impossible to cope, especially with looking after her four children properly. She found it easier to pour out her problems to the linkworker because they both spoke the same language, and the linkworker was able to understand, certainly more than the doctor.

Nasreen was persuaded by her sister-in-law to see her GP because she looked ill. She told him that she had lost her appetite and a lot of weight over a very short period of time. She also mentioned being unable to sleep well at night. It was only when the GP asked if there was anything worrying her that she told him, reluctantly and briefly, about disagreements with her parents over her marriage arrangements. She said she did not want to go into it with him because she did not think he could do anything to change the situation that was making her miserable. However, the doctor could give her sleeping pills to help her rest and sleep a bit more.

> I didn't want to tell him that I was having these problems at home, because I knew he couldn't do anything about it. He gave me vitamin tablets and sleeping pills because I said I couldn't eat or sleep properly.

Sunita kept going to see her GP with complaints such as pains in her back, tiredness, and not eating or sleeping well. Each time she went back, the symptoms seemed to have got worse. Finally, her GP asked her if everything was all right with her husband, or if there were any problems with the children. She told him then that her younger brother had recently died. It was only after some 'negotiation' that it became clear that it was the bereavement that was at the root of Sunita's ill-health.

Jaswinder saw her GP with her daughter, who explained that her mother's bad health had begun since her father threw them out of the house, and that she was very depressed. She spent so much time thinking about it all and crying all the time that she got terrible headaches, and became desperately tired. Jaswinder said that she couldn't stop herself from imagining all that could happen to her and her children. The doctor told her not to worry so much, and that thinking about it all would only make her feel worse.

> I explained I was feeling very weak and had dizzy spells. So the doctor gave me some iron tablets and said that I must take care that I ate enough. But I still felt weak, as if all the strength had left my body.

And I wasn't sleeping very well at night. I stopped going to the doctor because I didn't think he could give me a cure for my worries. He just said I musn't worry so much.

There was no doubt that the women were more direct and forthright about their problems when they spoke to an ICMHP worker, because they were able to talk in much greater depth. They were quite clear what their problem was, and realised that it helped to talk to someone about it.

I go to the Asian Drop-In Centre at the ICMHP. There I can talk to the workers and the other women who come there. It's very good for me.

It's good to talk to her (the ICMHP worker). It's good to talk about my family in Pakistan to another woman. She comes and sees me at home, which is nice — to have another woman in the house. I like women's company.

Seven of the women consulted the Inner City Mental Health Project (ICMHP) team about their depression or other disorders. Most were getting help for the first time. The women had been seen by an Asian female worker from the ICMHP, and/or had spoken to an Asian linkworker at the health centre. These were women workers who could speak Urdu, Punjabi, or other South Asian languages, and were available to help patients in their consultations with GPs, or at the ante-natal clinic. Funding for linkworkers has always been precarious, and linkworkers do a lot of hard and invaluable work for quite modest rates of pay. Because they share language and culture with the patients, they are often asked to help with a whole range of matters that are beyond their remit or particular expertise. This puts linkworkers under considerable stress, while highlighting the urgent need for a broadly-based counselling service.

Other sources of help were staff from the social services department and social workers who helped to sort out the women's housing problems and chronic money difficulties. Three of the women mentioned getting help from a social worker.

> The social worker went with me to get some money from the social
> security office, and helped us to get this house. She used to go to the
> housing department with us, and help with any problems the children
> had at school or anywhere else.

> The social services send a lady around to help with the cleaning. I
> couldn't do it on my own. She also helps me with the shopping,
> because I have lost the confidence to do a lot of things on my own.

Three of the women had suffered more severely than the others, and
had received hospital treatment. All of them said that this was
because their illness had got much worse. Jaswinder described her
experience in hospital —

> When I went into hospital I felt more anxious. I kept thinking, what
> sort of jail have they put me in. The doctors and nurses would come
> and give me tablets. I don't remember very much about being in hos-
> pital, only that I wanted to go home. I didn't have anyone to talk to at
> all there.

❧ Religious faith

All the women turned to their religion for help and comfort in various ways. This was plain in the way they expressed their understanding of illness and misfortune, and by the fact that they might decide
to visit a religious healer.

Most of the women mentioned 'the will of Allah' or 'Rab's will'
when talking about illness, death, or something they saw as fated or
predestined, and said that they prayed regularly. They understood
their illness or predicament as having been sent by Allah, and
expressed no resentment about it. But this does not mean they had
reconciled themselves to what had happened, and to the fact that
their fate was to be 'a life of tears'. Buddhists believe that the way to
truth lies through reconciliation with the burdens of life on earth.
The Islamic and Sikh traditions do not subscribe to this philosophy,
even though pain may be seen as Allah's (or Rab's) will. Needless to
say, these are highly complex religious philosophies, and it is not

possible to begin to explore them here, but certain themes emerge through some of the things the women said —

> I know that his life was written by Allah only for so long, but ever since he died my life has been full of sorrow.

> Only Allah and I know what's happening to me. That's how deep my pain goes. The thing is I don't know when it will all end, because there's no cure for this illness except from Allah. That's why, although I didn't pray before, I do now, all the time, asking Allah to please give me some rest.

> We pray five times a day and also recite the Koran. It makes me feel better, because I think there's nothing for me but to pray that I get better.

> Honestly, I wouldn't be able to get up in the mornings if I didn't make myself get up to read the prayers ... I spend a lot of time just sitting and reading the Koran, and I try to pray five times a day, because that gives me more support than all these tablets I take.

For Jamila, her troubles and fears were very closely tied to her religious beliefs and practices. She was convinced that, somehow, 'religious' or 'magical' powers were being used against her. It was evident that in her case — and others like hers — anyone trying to help or give advice would, at the very least, need a basic understanding of the religious and cultural traditions involved.

The Inner City Mental Health Project

Most of the women who received help from statutory caring agencies were referred to them by their GPs, or as a result of outreach work by Asian mental health professionals. It is significant that in the three years of developing mental health services for Asian people in inner Bristol through the ICMHP team, more than half the Asian clients (54%) referred to them had had no previous help or support for their problems, either from statutory or voluntary sector agencies.

Three kinds of service were offered to Asian people:

- Counselling and therapy at a health centre used by most of the local Asian communities.

- Counselling and therapy in people's own homes.

- Drop-in facilities.

All the services were provided by Asian workers with psychiatric and nursing experience, as well as the relevant language skills.

Table 1 gives a breakdown of the 98 referrals to ICMHP over a two-year period, by agency. Virtually all the referrals by GPs and health visitors – and even some from psychiatrists and community psychiatric nurses – came from the health centre, where an Asian worker from ICMHP offered regular sessions. In short, the Asian worker's regular involvement at the health centre generated about 40 per cent of all referrals over two years. There are several advantages to this:

- It offers the opportunity to have informal chats with the

patients, work closely with GPs, and help them pick up signs of distress.

- From the patient's point of view, physical and mental suffering are closely related, and it is better (and less stigmatising) to deal with both at the same time.

- It gives the Asian worker the opportunity to work closely with other health workers such as health visitors and midwives. This cuts out delay, and helps build up a more integrated service.

Table 1. Referrals to ICMHP over two years, by agency

	No.	%
GP	25	26
Social worker	12	12
Community psychiatric nurse	6	6
Psychiatrist	11	11
Relative	3	3
Self	15	15
Probation service	1	1
Hostel staff	3	3
Health visitor	11	11
Psychiatric hospital	2	2
Other team members	1	1
Other	8	8

Home visits were an important part of the care offered to Asians — 43 per cent of the work with them took place in their own homes. As the study shows, many of the women were isolated, and were unable or reluctant to visit a health centre. A majority of the sessions involved counselling.

The advantages of working with the women in their own homes were numerous —

- It gave the health worker the chance to see the women in their own surroundings, where they could talk more openly and intimately, to assess their domestic circumstances, and also to meet other members of the family.

- From the women's point of view, the fact that the worker had made the effort to see them at home was often a sign that she was serious and sincere about trying to help.

- It meant that appointments were fairly easy to make, as the women did not have to travel to see the worker.

Once the women were ready to socialise more, they could use the project team's services at the drop-in centre. This was staffed by three Asian workers with a variety of language skills, and offered therapeutic and recreational activities. Mothers could use creche facilities while they were there, and transport was provided. While the project team's services were open to both men and women, it was the women who used them more. Table 2 shows who used the project team's services over a two-year period, by age and sex. Over half the women seen had been diagnosed as suffering from either major or minor depression.

In many cases, health and social services workers visited the women together, and were able to draw on each others' skills, knowledge and resources. This kind of close cooperation seems to be the best way in which statutory agencies can address the wide range of social and health needs involved in these cases.

Table 2. Project team users, by age and sex,
over two years.

Age	Male		Female		Total	
	No.	%	No.	%	No.	%
Under 16	0	0	1	1	1	1
16-29	3	3	26	27	29	30
30-45	11	11	24	24	35	36
46-60/65	7	7	16	16	23	23
60/65 and over	2	2	8	8	10	10
Total	23	23	75	76	98	100

Recommendations

It cannot be emphasised too strongly that health authorities and social services departments have a duty to provide for everyone in their catchment area. The needs of small, localised ethnic communities are no less important than those of the majority of the population. What this means, first of all, is knowing what those needs are or might be – the nature and size of the different communities, how many among them do not speak or understand English, etc – and then, accordingly, planning, delivering and publicising a comprehensive service. This might include the following steps:

- Building a counselling service into the GP consultation, with ethnic minority counsellors included in the team whenever they are needed. All the evidence suggests that Asians are reluctant to use mental health services. But GPs and other medical services tend to be well used, and are usually the first port of call for those suffering from depression. It is very important that every step is taken to detect psychological stress at the primary health care stage, and to ensure that the patient is referred to a specialist if necessary. It is also important to explain, carefully and fully, if any medication is prescribed, what it is for, what it can and cannot do, and to urge patients to return if their symptoms persist. Finally, it would be useful if GPs were able to understand a few key phrases in the main languages used by those on their lists. Some of the women said how pleased they were when they found that a GP had taken the trouble to learn a few Punjabi terms for common symptoms and parts of the body.

- Improving opportunities for joint consultations by health and social service workers, so that they can cooperate on a case.

- Improving links between health and social workers and housing department officers.

- Training social workers in the cultures and needs of the different communities they are caring for.

- Translating any relevant information about different health and social services.

- Employing properly qualified interpreters, and making sure that their services are available in health centres and GP practices.

- Taking account of difficulties the women may have in visiting the health centre or surgery by providing home counselling facilities.

- Setting up special drop-in centres for particular ethnic groups.

- Making health centres and hospitals less daunting places, and accessible to people from all ethnic groups.

- Working with local women's and community groups to bring women together so that they can talk to each other about common problems.

The CRE has recently produced a code of practice in primary health care, which has been endorsed by the Health Secretary. Three further codes are currently being prepared on mental health, maternity services, and social services, and should provide indispensable guidance to all agencies concerned with the health and social service needs of ethnic minority communities.

The *Code of Practice in Rented Housing* (CRE, 1991), and a new guide on ethnic monitoring in housing, *Accounting for Equality* (CRE, 1991), will help councils ensure that they do not treat applicants for housing services differently because of their race, colour, nationality or ethnic origin. Both these publications, as well as the CRE's report on racial violence and harassment in housing, *Living in Terror* (CRE,1987), give advice on the procedures that should be adopted for dealing with complaints of racial harassment.

COMMISSION FOR RACIAL EQUALITY

The Commission for Racial Equality was set up by the Race Relations Act 1976 with the duties of:

- Working towards the elimination of discrimination.

- Promoting equality of opportunity and good relations between persons of different racial groups.

- Keeping under review the working of the Act, and, when required by the Secretary of State or when it otherwise thinks it is necessary, drawing up and submitting to the Secretary of State proposals for amending it.

London (Head Office)

Elliot House
10-12 Allington Street
London SW1E 5EH
☎ 071-828 7022

Birmingham

Alpha Tower (11th floor)
Suffolk Street Queensway
Birmingham B1 1TT
☎ 021-632 4544

Leeds

Yorkshire Bank Chambers
(1st floor)
Infirmary Street
Leeds LS1 2JP
☎ 0532-434413

Manchester

Maybrook House (5th floor)
40 Blackfriars Street
Manchester M3 2EG
☎ 061-831 7782

Leicester

Haymarket House (4th floor)
Haymarket Shopping Centre
Leicester LE1 3YG
☎ 0533-517852

Scotland

100 Princes Street
Edinburgh EH2 3AA
☎ 031-226 5186